EXPLORING

freshwater
habitats

Written by Diane Snowball
Wildlife illustrations by Cynthia A. Belcher
Cartoon illustrations by Miriam Katin

Red fox and snapping turtle   page 20

Egret   page 8

Cypress swamp   page 19

Sculpin and shrimp   page 13

Contents

Hippopotamus and Nile monitor   page 5

Raccoon   page 15

Rivers

Mediterranean Sea

Africa

Indian Ocean

The Nile River in Africa begins in the mountains and flows 4,145 miles to the Mediterranean Sea. On the way, it passes through vast plains and steaming tropical forests. This river helps keep many kinds of African wildlife alive.

papyrus

hammerhead stork

nest

People have lived along the Nile River for over 100,000 years. It provides both food and transportation.

3

An African fish eagle glides down to snatch a large fish from the water.

A Nile crocodile warns other animals to stay away by sunbathing with its mouth open.

The soft-shelled turtle has blood vessels in the skin over its shell to help it breathe.

giant Nile perch

papyrus

kingfisher

flamingos

shoe-billed stork

A marsh mongoose looks for bird and reptile eggs along the riverbank.

The hippopotamus weighs about 7,000 pounds, but underwater it is graceful and lightfooted, almost dancing along.

Nile monitor lizard

The giant Nile perch can weigh 350 pounds and be over 3 feet long.

A carp is picking bits of food off the hippo's skin.

5

Food chains

Many other plants and animals live along the Nile River. Each animal depends on other animals or plants in the area for food.

For example:

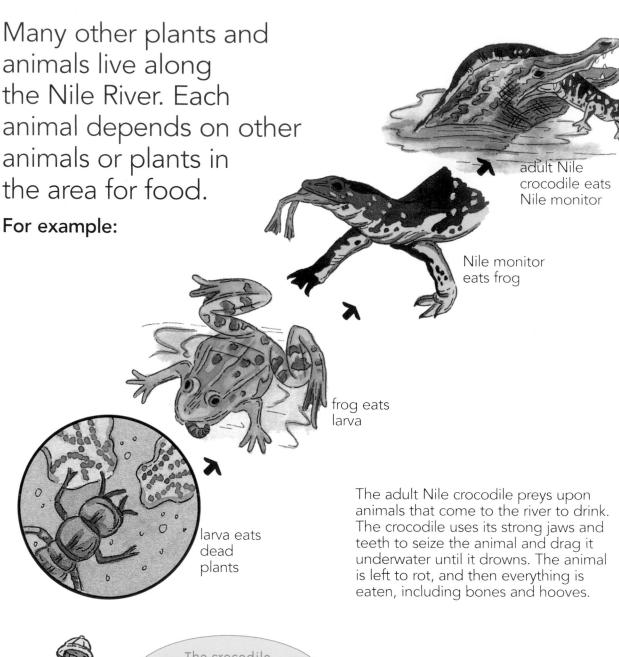

adult Nile crocodile eats Nile monitor

Nile monitor eats frog

frog eats larva

larva eats dead plants

The adult Nile crocodile preys upon animals that come to the river to drink. The crocodile uses its strong jaws and teeth to seize the animal and drag it underwater until it drowns. The animal is left to rot, and then everything is eaten, including bones and hooves.

The crocodile swallows pebbles because they help it digest food.

CAN YOU FIND IT?

Turn back the page and find the electric catfish.

6

Marshes

Marshes are wetlands where grasses or sedges grow. In one part of the Florida Everglades, a sedge called saw grass grows so thickly it looks like a golden ocean. During the wet season, shallow water gently moves through the area in one large sheet, and the marsh is full of life.

United States

Atlantic Ocean

Florida, U.S.A.

strangler vine

Once there were a million alligators and several million wading birds in the Everglades. Now there are only a few thousand because people have killed the animals and used the water.

saw grass blade

egret

marsh rabbit

saw grass

alligator

A dragonfly, with wings spread like an airplane's, waits to catch mosquitoes and deer flies.

An alligator lies in the sun to warm its body.

Alligators bellow at each other at mating time. They arch their heads and tails, breathe in, and make air vibrate in their throats.

egret

Apple snails glide underwater and rise to breathe through their snorkel-like tubes.

lily pads and flowers

pig frog

saw grass

8

rushes

A snail kite hovers over the water, looking for apple snails to eat.

Deer slosh through the marsh to eat saw grass that has edges as sharp as broken glass

apple snail eggs

The bladderwort is a plant with no roots. It sucks in a souplike meal for food.

9

Food chains

Many other plants and animals live in the Florida saw grass marsh. Each animal depends on other animals or plants in the area for food.

For example:

wood stork eats mosquito fish

mosquito fish eats cyclops

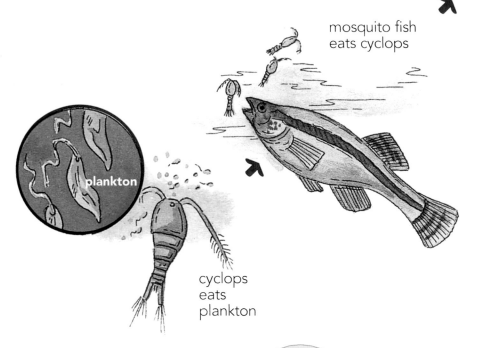

plankton

cyclops eats plankton

Wood storks grope along in shallow water with their beaks partly open but snap them closed when they touch a fish. The speed of this snap is amazing. It is faster than the time it takes for a light to come on when you flip the switch.

200lb 130lb 440lb 40lb 43lb 20lb 7lb

At nesting time, a stork family with tow young ones eats about 440 pounds of fish in four months.

CAN YOU FIND IT?

Turn back the page and find the green tree frog.

10

Lakes

Lakes are big deep holes in the Earth filled with fresh water. One of the biggest is Lake Baikal in Russia. It is 400 miles wide and 5,380 feet deep and holds more water than any other lake on our planet. Lake Baikal originally formed from the sea, so its inhabitants are more like sea creatures than those in other lakes.

summer

Lake Baikal is 25 million years old. Even in the summer, its water temperature is only 38°F, so divers have to wear thermal underwear under their diving suits.

whooping swan

You can see right through comephorus fish. They are completely transparent.

salmon

Sponges grow close together and look like large green carpets.

In winter, a 3-foot-thick layer of ice covers the lake. Baikal seals stay in the water because it's warmer than the air. They breathe through holes in the ice.

Tiny snails creep over plants looking for a meal.

perch

Lake Baikal

Russia

Mongolia

China

The Baikal seal is the only freshwater seal.

pike

encrusting sponges

The sculpin gives birth to baby fish rather than releasing eggs and sperm, the way other fish do.

The shrimp has antennae, hairy legs, and a segmented body.

13

Food chains

Many other plants and animals live in Lake Baikal. Each animal depends on other animals or plants in the area for food.

For example:

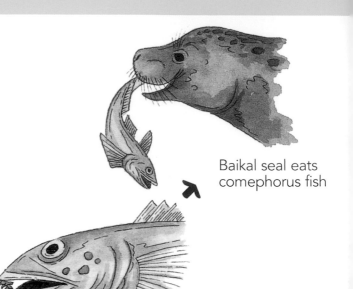

Baikal seal eats comephorus fish

comephorus fish eats shrimp

shrimp eats copepod

Seals do most of their eating at twilight or during the night. They can dive for 25 minutes to depths of 500 feet to find comephorus and other fish to eat.

copepod eats plankton

plankton

CAN YOU FIND IT?

Turn back the page and find the whitefish.

Pregnant seals do not spend the winter in the water. They deliver their young in snow dens on the ice and feed them until they are about two months old.

MATERNITY

MATERNITY

Streams

A stream is a body of running water smaller than a river. It usually contains waterfalls, pools, and rapids. Different plants and animals live in each part because of the speed of the water and the type of ground beneath it. There are many streams in southeastern Canada.

waterfall

skunk

pool

trout

raccoon

In a stream, a thousand animals can live in an area just four times the size of your head. They are attached to the floor of the stream so that the current does not carry them away.

A trout can jump completely out of the water to snatch a hovering insect.

A darter darts to the surface to catch an insect and then settles back to the bottom where the water does not move so fast.

Water pennies cling to the rocks with their sucker disks.

stoneflies

water penny

spotted salamander

snail

16

The blackfly larvae spin a silken rug on a rock and sink strong hooks into it.

To trap food, the caddisfly larva spins a silken net shaped like a sack.

The stonefly larva spends between one and three years in the water before emerging as an adult. Then it immediately mates, lays eggs, and dies.

frog

blackfly larvae

caddisfly larva net

stonefly larva

pond weed

Female trout make shallow nests in the gravel to lay eggs, which the male fertilizes. After the female covers the fertilized eggs, they are left alone to develop and hatch into tiny fish.

Food chains

Many other plants and animals live in Canadian streams. Each animal depends on other animals or plants in the area for food.

For example:

raccoon eats crayfish

crayfish eats leaf matter

The raccoon's diet changes during the year, depending on what is available. In the summer, it especially likes crayfish. Even when a crayfish pinches a raccoon with its claws, the raccoon just keeps on eating.

By the end of the winter, raccoons may weigh only half as much as they did in the summer. Even their feet look shriveled!

CAN YOU FIND IT?

Turn back the page and find the mudpuppy.

Cypress swamps

There is an eeriness about cypress swamps. These wetlands are filled with twisting channels of dark water and giant baldcypress trees looming overhead. Many rare and endangered species depend on wetlands like the Maryland cypress swamp.

needles

seed ball

buttresses

knees

stinkpot turtle

WATER SAMPLE

One baldcypress in Maryland is about 500 years old. Its roots and knees form a platform at the bank of the river.

copperhead snake

19

An osprey nests in a dead pine tree at the edge of the swamp.

A belted kingfisher plunges into the murky water to catch a fish.

A snapping turtle lays its eggs on dry land.

Arcadian flycatcher

wood ducks

red fox

minnows

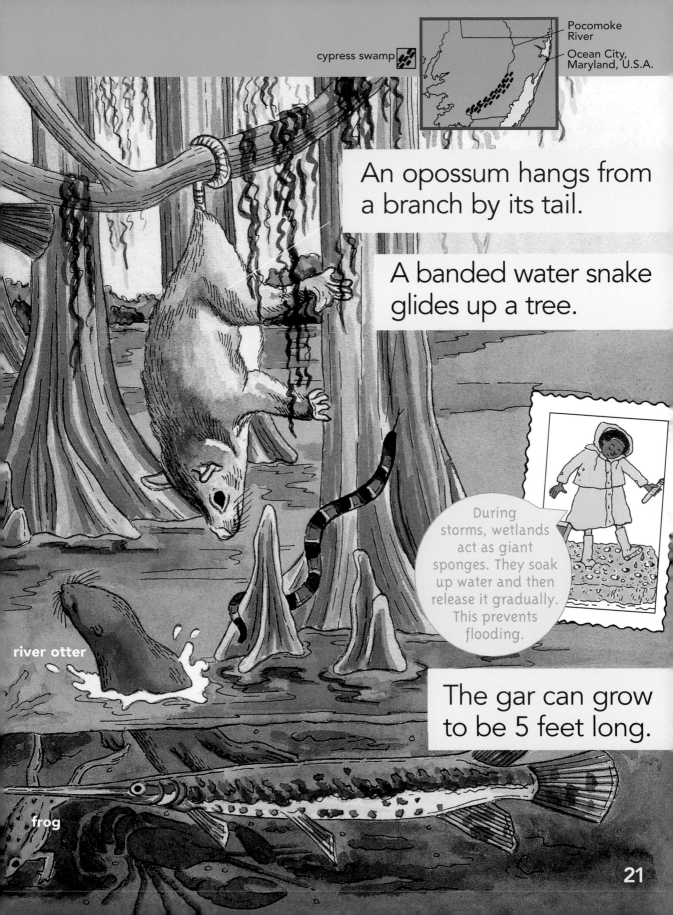

cypress swamp

Pocomoke River

Ocean City, Maryland, U.S.A.

An opossum hangs from a branch by its tail.

A banded water snake glides up a tree.

During storms, wetlands act as giant sponges. They soak up water and then release it gradually. This prevents flooding.

river otter

The gar can grow to be 5 feet long.

frog

21

Many other plants and animals live in the Maryland cypress swamp. Each animal depends on other animals or plants in the area for food.

For example:

belted kingfisher eats fish

fish eats mosquito larvae

mosquito larva eats algae

The belted kingfisher can dive from a branch to seize a fish in the water. It also can hover in the air 20 to 40 feet above the water and then dive straight down or in a spiral. It returns to its perch, beats the fish on the branch, tosses the fish in the air, and swallows it headfirst.

The kingfisher is one of the few birds that dives headfirst into water.

CAN YOU FIND IT?

Turn back the page and find the crayfish.

Glossary

algae - plants that grow in the water. They do not have stems, roots, or leaves and can make their own food.

baldcypress - a conifer tree that grows in swamps. It is deciduous, so it loses its leaves in the fall.

blood vessels - tubes carrying blood to and from the heart.

buttress - a spreading, fanlike growth at the base of a tree trunk. It helps support the tree.

copepod - a group of very small animals that lives in water. This large group of animals is an important food source for other freshwater and saltwater animals.

fertilized egg - an egg that has combined with a sperm and can develop into an animal.

food chain - the path of food energy. It usually goes from plants to plant-eating animals to animals that eat other animals.

freshwater - water that is not salty.

habitat - the place where a plant or an animal lives.

larva - the wormlike stage in an insect's development, after it hatches from the egg. More than one larva are called "larvae."

plankton - the mass of tiny plants and animals that floats in water.

prey - to hunt other animals for food. It also can mean the animal that is hunted.

reptile - a cold-blooded animal that has a backbone and scales and that lays eggs. It crawls on its belly or creeps on short legs. Snakes, lizards, alligators, crocodiles, and turtles are reptiles.

sedge - a wetland plant like grass, with firm long leaves that have tiny sharp teeth along their edges.

segmented - marked or divided into parts.

species - a group of plants or animals that are alike in certain ways.

swamp - an area of wetland that is often partly covered with water.

thermal - designed to help hold in body heat. Clothes made of loosely-knit material with air spaces are thermal.

tropical - in the area of the earth called the tropics, where the climate is hot and there are heavy rains.

tropics - the strip of the earth around the equator. It stretches from the Tropic of Cancer to the Tropic of Capricorn.

wetlands - land under water or with wet soil for a minimum of two weeks a year. A swamp is one kind of wetland.

Index